Folklore Galore

Folk Practices from Long Ago

Sylvester Ayre

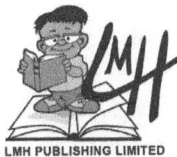

LMH PUBLISHING LIMITED

Editor: K. Sean Harris
Cover design: Sanya Dockery
Typeset & book layout: Sanya Dockery

Published by: LMH Publishing Limited
Suite 10 -11, Sagicor Industrial Park
7 Norman Road, Kingston C.S.O., Jamaica
Tel.: (876) 938-0005; Fax: (876) 759-8752
Email: lmhbookpublishing@cwjamaica.com
Website: www.lmhpublishing.com

Printed in the U.S.A.   ISBN: 978-976-8245-51-9

NATIONAL LIBRARY OF JAMAICA CATALOGUING-IN-PUBLICATION DATA

Ayre, Sylvester
    Folklore galore: folk practices from long time ago / Sylvester Ayre

      p. : ill. , cm
ISBN 978-976-8245-51-9 (pbk)

Folklore – Jamaica   2. Jamaica – Social life and customs

398   dc 23

Content

Beliefs, Myths & Remedies

How To Know One's Future Spouse

In order to experience a premonition of whomsoever one's future spouse will be, it is advised by folk 'mystics' of old, that the seeker should eat an extra large mouthful of salted codfish just before retiring to sleep, on any chosen night.

The seeker, also, should not drink water after having eaten the salted codfish, despite the upsurge of thirst that is expected to come before he/she goes to sleep.

During sleep, it is said, a dream will unfold. The dream will reveal a clear picture of one's future spouse, most likely carrying a glassful of water.

But, should the form of no one appear in a dream, or should there be no relevant dream, it could mean that no Mr. Right or Miss Born-For-Me is yet lounging in the precincts of romance.

Love-Bush

Its name is 'dodder' but most folks call it 'love-bush'. Dodder is a parasite. It is a kind of brusque that has many long, yellowish tentacles growing out from its moorings on the sap of trees and bush.

Apart from its medicinal value as a proven remedy with which to treat gripe in infants, dodder's role as love-bush is intended to prove whether one's love for another person is duly reciprocated.

The practice of propagating love-bush for such a purpose was popular among young folks, including school children. Several decades ago the culture of courtship was still heavily influenced by romantic notions.

The seeker of his/her love's answer is required to pick a twig of love-bush and take it to an appropriate shrub or small tree. Before tossing the twig of love-bush to the chosen shrub/tree the following incantation must be spoken while focusing one's mind strongly on the loved one involved.

"I love thee true, do ye love me too?"

That incantation must be repeated three times.

An answer to this lover's question depends on whether the twig of love-bush grows or not. It is said that if the love-bush does not grow over a given time it is a sure indication that one's love is not being reciprocated. But if the love-bush grows and flourishes, it indicates that love is flowing well both ways.

Guilt or Innocence

In Jamaican folk culture there are mysterious ways of determining whether someone accused of theft is guilty or not. One method of finding out who the thief is (whenever theft has been reported by someone) is the use of a bible and a house door key along with an utterance of prescribed words.

The following method is merely another one that accomplishes, basically, the same result – to affirm the guilt or innocence of someone suspected of having committed a theft. The possible innocence of the accused will nullify this occultation. Justice (according to folk sages of antiquity) starts when a glassful of water is placed on a level surface.

A gold ring hanging by an appropriate length of thread or a long strand of hair held firmly between one's thumb and forefinger, must be lowered or submerged into the glass of water. The hanging ring thereby becomes a pendulum.

A steady hand is required to keep the hanging ring clear of the bottom and sides of the glass so that expected movement by this pendulum is not activated by a shaking hand.

While steadily holding the thread-and-ring pendulum into the glass of water the following incantation must be said:

"By Saint Peter
By Saint Paul,
By the true and
Living God:
Tom is the thief."

Should Tom be innocent of the accusation, the expected miracle will not unfold. But if Tom is indeed guilty of theft, the pendulum will start its own movement by swinging from one side of the glass of water to the other.

The swinging pendulum, if allowed, usually develops a velocity strong enough to break the glass that is hit harder and harder by the swinging ring.

It is believed, to this day, that this is an infallible way of proving guilt or innocence.

To Get The Judge's Favour

No matter how modern the world becomes there are folks everywhere who still observe ancient beliefs and primitive practices.

Faith in the occult, for example, has never become obsolete despite the advancement of science and technology. Does it not seem incredible that in this scientific age it is still practised and believed by many people, that a mere twig or a small plant can influence a judge's final verdict concerning a case being tried in a court of law?

It is advised, by folk practitioners, that a judge's decision in court will be swayed in favour of the litigant who has a small plant of Madam Fate wrapped into a handkerchief carried on the person to court. The litigant must also keep in mind, sentiments contained in Psalms 27, verses 12 and 13.

Verse 12: "Deliver me not over unto mine enemies: for false witnesses are risen up against me and such as breathe out cruelty."

Verse 13: "I had fainted, unless I had believed to see the goodness of the Lord in the land of the living."

It is said that several court cases have been decided in favour of the litigants who had Madam Fate.

To Control Stray-Prone Dogs

I once had a couple of dogs that mysteriously vanished from home leaving no trace of their whereabouts. Weeks later they came back home panting and looking tired and famished. They did that disappearing act three times over a few years. I didn't like it at all.

Apparently, that kind of dog-gone act had been occurring since the days of antiquity as evidenced by the fact that folk of olden times devised a mysterious way of forcing dogs to stay at home without an urge to wander.

Old folklore advises that dogs possessed with wander-lust should be "measured" by using a length of stick cut from a cassava plant. With the cassava stick, measure from the tip of each dog's nose to the end of its tail. The stick must thereafter be buried underground within the confines of the dog's home. It is known that dogs so treated will surely lose the instinct to stray again. I did it and it worked well. It is also known that if dogs are fed regularly with strongly brewed coffee they become fierce. Dogs may become dangerous, even to their masters, if regularly fed with brewed marijuana.

No More Flogging

In the following lore Florence, now in her late 60's, reminisces about what she was advised to do in order to avoid the punishment – usually flogging – inflicted by her aunt or her aunt's husband, both of whom acted as Florence's guardians during her years of growing up in a deep country village in St. Catherine, Jamaica.

Young Florence knew that staying out of her home at night time would earn for herself a severe flogging every time. Getting a whipping each time she violated the strict rules of her so-called guardians was as sure as getting wet when one stands in falling rain.

Nevertheless, as a healthy teenager then, full of life and energy to expend, even the ominous threat of the beating could not totally inhibit her insatiable appetite for fun and social interactions with folks around the neighbourhood and the wider society as enjoyed by her peers.

Florence sometimes boldly rebelled against the unreasonable restrictions placed against her. She would, at times, decide to take the punishment rather than not having attended the annual 'orchestra' dance at the schoolroom.

She would also break the taboo sometimes and go out to meet her boyfriend, knowing fully well what the penalty would be when she returned home.

Even at the age of 16 years, Florence was still subjected to flogging for whatever reason cited by her torturers.

Then, one day an old lady who lived in the neighbourhood since her day of birth, told Florence about her own experience of whipping by her father during her childhood. The old lady, in deep sympathy with Florence's plight, offered her advice which she had learnt from someone who saw her suffering administered unreservedly by her father many years ago.

Yet, it was only when the old lady said: "De advice work like magic", that instantly caught Florence's full attention. The question sprang to her mind: *What could be done that, according to the old lady, would prevent her aunt and her husband from battering her at every drop of a hat?*

The old lady further deepened Florence's interest by saying: "Afta me tek de advice and do what it seh, me father just stop beatin' me..."

THE ADVICE

The advice given was that Florence should, whenever a flogging was anticipated, pull from the ground at least three units of a bush called chick-weed or iron-weed which could be about 18 inches or taller in height.

This species of wild bush grows profusely at certain locations in St. Catherine and some other parishes. Chick-weed is said to contain powerful medicinal potential.

METHOD

Lay the three or more units of chick-weed together length-wise and wrap them around the palm of a hand to fold and become a circle that is known as 'cotter'. The usual role of a cotter is to be used as a cushion placed on the head of someone carrying a heavy load thereon. Cotter can be made of differing types of materials such as cloth, grass, dried banana fronds etc.

Fasten securely the ends of the chick-weed plants so that unfolding of the cotter may not occur. Place the cotter on the ground out of harm's way. Put on top of the cotter a stone heavy enough to prevent any slippage of its form. The stone also forms part of the ritual.

That done, walk away towards home in the firm assurance that the spell cast by the cotter and stone will de-spirit the torturers. Such a spell was cast time and again by Florence. The expected result was achieved every time. No more flogging for Florence from then onward.

Blessed Donkey

It is believed by some folks that the hairless dark sports found at the upper part, between both front legs near the chest of all donkeys, originated from miraculous finger touches by Jesus Christ, done as marks that symbolized his blessing on the donkey for the safe and comfortable ride that the beast provided during his triumphal entry into Jerusalem on Palm Sunday.

He had previously endured a less tranquil ride on a mule, it is said. It is believed too that those spots referred to on the donkey constitute a sort of dynamo-generator which provides subtle light that helps donkeys to see well if they have to move about in the darkness of night.

Did you know...that donkeys take thirteen months to develop and give birth to their offsprings?

That mules do not reproduce themselves?

That mules have little or no involvement with mating?

That a mule is propagated when a female donkey is mated with a horse?

That when a male donkey is mated with a female horse the offspring becomes not a horse, donkey nor mule, but a hybrid beast known as 'mule-royal'?

That if a male horse is blindfoldedly mated with its mother, the horse on realizing the fact of mating with its mother, will use its teeth to rip away its male organs and bear the consequence – death?

Folk Customs of Death

Folk customs relating to death are many in the Caribbean. One of the several old folk customs still observed to a lesser extent than in the past was designed originally to prevent the spirit, or what Jamaicans call duppy, of a recently departed spouse from coming back to haunt the surviving spouse.

It is believed, by some folks, that the spirit of say, an arrogant, miserable, departed spouse, is most likely to return and try to perpetuate deeds that he/she had practised during life.

The living spouse may, therefore, want to act pre-emptively in order to discourage possible spirit visitations at the survivor's bedroom. Widows, particularly, often tell tales of sex-seeking spirits of departed husbands.

The following is a ritual that may be performed, according to folk sages of long ago, after a spouse has died at home leaving the remaining spouse with a keen desire to keep his/her spirit at bay forever.

THE RITUAL

The living spouse should have in hand a broom which must be used to sweep along the path walked by carriers of the dead spouse's body while on route out of the house.

Sweeping with the broom ought to continue until the door-way or the bottom-most step is reached outdoors.

That simple act, it is said, symbolically ushers the spirit of the dead out of the house permanently.

"...me neva see no sign a me wife spirit," said Mr. Campbell, a farmer of St. Catherine, who performed that ritual right after the death of his wife two years earlier. "An' me don't even get a dream from har," he declared triumphantly.

To Become Pregnant

There are many women who are disappointed by their state of prolonged childlessness. Each of them seems willing to do almost anything possible to become pregnant and give birth to a child. But fate has, so far, not been kind to them in that regard.

There also are women who do not have the biological completeness to conceive a child. Others have the biological structures to become pregnant and reproduce except for a relatively simple problem that is commonly described in folk parlance as 'blockage of the tubes' in the reproductive system.

Advice to women in this position has come from folk doctors, who through the ages past, have recommended the use of 'dog-blood' as a treatment to remove infectious impediments from the 'tubes'.

Let it be hastily explained that 'dog-blood' is the name given to a small plant growing in the wild in small colonies some places in the countryside. The plants, having small leaves, grow to an average height of eighteen inches. At certain times they bear many tiny, green berries that, in time, become red as they ripen. Using dog-blood is simple.

METHOD:

Pull up from the ground one, two or three (depending on size) dog-blood plants. Wash earth off the root and cut the plant or plants into bits before placing them into a quart of boiling water.

Let boiling continue for fifteen minutes. Take the brew from the fire and let it stand to cool before straining it. Take that decoction orally; a cupful in the morning and another in the evening. Repeat the process for at least nine consecutive days along with regular sexual intercourse until pregnancy occurs.

To Induce Birth Pains

It is unlikely that there is anyone who likes to endure severe pain. However, a pregnant female may feel a degree of concern if birth pains do not begin at the time expected.

Whenever that happens an expectant mother may prepare herself to visit a doctor in order to obtain induced pain which precedes the natural birth of all babies.

But in long past times, when medical doctors were not readily available, particularly in deep, rural parts of the country, a nana (midwife) would use home-grown remedies to induce pre-birth pains in the mother-to-be, when necessary.

One of the foremost remedies used in those days consisted of two ingredients, namely-castor oil and 'tea' brewed from the boiling of thyme. A tablespoon of castor-oil was given to the mother-to-be. That dose of castor-oil would activate the pain before the 'tea', brewed from thyme, was given in order to enhance the coming of regular surges of labour pains preceding delivery of the baby.

Abortion by Bannabis

Bannabis is a species of the bean family. These edible beans are said to be very nutritious. Bannabis plants grow in the typical way of beans. They have vines that climb up on stakes or nearby trees. In time they bear pods filled with bean seeds that later reach maturity for eating.

But bannabis harbours a dark, age-old stigma which says that it is an abortifacient. In order to validate this long standing stigma, Ms. Florence Ashwood told of her own experience of what bannabis really is in relation to the abortion of pregnancies. The adverse effect of bannabis beans also applies to breeding female animals such as goats, cattle, donkeys etc. that might eat the growing bannabis plants.

Ms. Ashwood admitted to having heard a long time ago, about bannabis as an abortifacient. But apart from not having taken seriously that sort of folkloric advice, she further thought that any possible harm would come by way of the eating but not by just handling the stuff.

One day she visited the home of a friend. She assisted her friend to 'shell' bannabis beans to be cooked for dinner that evening. Ms. Ashwood said that her pregnancy was just at two months old. The beans she shelled were placed into her lap.

Ms. Ashwood knew not what her fate would be just hours later. She complained, late in the night, of having an unusual feeling inside of herself, followed by haemorrhaging. At daylight next morning she was taken to a medical doctor who confirmed that an abortion of her foetus had occurred.

What is the apparent mystery about bannabis that purportedly causes abortion of pregnancies? The answer, my friend, is blowing in the wind.

Strong Penile Erection

Folk remedies decocted from wild herbs, roots, barks, etc. have traditionally been used in Jamaica to enhance the performance of sexual intercourse. For men who are sexually dejuvinated or just tired, perhaps through excessive physical performances, the following remedy is made of three species of herbs, identified by their folk names: chick-weed, medina and duppy-gun. Duppy-gun is so called because of the multiple mini-explosions heard during the boiling of the weed. An amount of 10 ounces of the combined herbs mentioned must be garnered.

The herbs are found mainly in the country areas. A brew made from these herbs becomes an aphrodisiac reputed for strengthening of penile erection and improving the functions of the body. The combined herbs should be placed in boiling water and allowed to boil for 20 minutes. When cool, mix brew with a common sense amount of wine as a preservative.

Sweetened or not, a small wine-glassful of this brew should be taken orally each morning for nine consecutive mornings, as recommended by practitioners of folk cultural medicine.

This remedy is said to be a tried means of enhancing penile erection if no underlying illnesses negates the process.

Ringworm

Ringworm is classified as any of several contagious diseases of the skin, hair or nails of man and domestic animals, caused by fungi and characterized by ring-shaped discoloured patches of the skin that are covered with vesicles and scales.

Medication to treat ringworm can be obtained at any pharmacy. It is sold without a doctor's prescription.

However, there's also an effective folk remedy for ringworm. It can be obtained virtually free of cost, perhaps without having to leave one's home to get treatment.

Among the medicinal uses ascribed to garlic, the following one has invariably proven its effectiveness.

METHOD:
Cut diametrically a clove of garlic and use any of the cut ends (on which juice is seen) to rub the patch of ringworm

at whatever part of one's body that is so affected. Repeat treatment if necessary. The ringworm will die within a couple of days.

Against Sinusitis

Among other folk remedies recommended as treatment for sinusitis is the use of a plant called periwinkle in Jamaica; one that produces flowers with mauve colouration while the other blooms white petals.

It is the one bearing white blooms that is reputed to hold the treatment or possible cure for sinusitis.

An experience has been related in which a young man was, from childhood, badly affected by what his doctor said was sinusitis; so badly affected was he with the disease, that pus draining from his facial canals oozed out through his nostrils and ears while giving off an unpleasant odour despite treatment by doctors over a period of years.

Then someone came along and gave simple advice. He was told to put seven white flowers of periwinkle into boiling water and let them boil for 10 minutes. When cooled, the resultant brew must be taken once daily.

The young man carried out the process and repeated same for several weeks. He was told also to use no vessel or utensils made of aluminium in the process. Today, sinusitis, for him, is only a memory.

Against Gastritis

Folk remedies with a twist of mystery are common all over the country, especially in deep rural parts. The following remedy is of such an ilk. Acute gastritis often defies medical treatments to bring cure to this ailment. However, folk doctors have prescribed a remedy that is said to be a proven and effective treatment to eliminate the discomfort experienced by persons afflicted with gastritis.

An informant, Mr. Leaford Burke, told of the ingredients and method used in preparing this remedy as passed down through the ages from ancestors.

Ingredients:

Five sour or Seville oranges, three fronds of single-bible (aloe vera) and half a pint of white proof rum.

Method:

Cut the fronds of single-bible into small bits. Cut each Seville orange into halves. The apparent mystery is that one half of each of the five Seville oranges should be thrown away. The other five halves, along with the bits of single-bible, must be placed into a pot containing two quarts of boiling water. Boiling of that concoction should last until the liquid in the pot is reduced to one and a half quarts.

The boiled decoction should be taken from the fire and allowed to cool. When cool, the white proof rum should be added to the mixture.

Shake it well to enable integration of all ingredients. Have this concoction bottled and stored in a cool place.

The relief or cure from gastritis will more than compensate for the inherent bitterish taste of the medicine.

A small glassful should be taken daily.

Tonsillitis

Folks call it 'skellion-grass'. It grows up from relatively deep into the ground and sends up 2-6 long fronds, averaging 12 inches above ground. The body of a single skellion-grass plant when fully grown is the size of the little finger of an average person's hand.

However, the important medicinal part of skellion-grass lies underground. There is an enlargement of its bottom in the ground. It is shaped as a small electrical light bulb. Inside of that bulbous part of skellion-grass there is a brightly coloured yellow kernel. That kernel of the skellion-grass can be reaped, (as it was in long gone days of our ancestors) placed into boiling water for fifteen minutes and used when cool as a gargle whenever someone is afflicted with tonsillitis. This remedy is said to have a strong healing effect on ailing, painful tonsils.

A Waste of Precious Blood

In her earlier years of life in London, England, Mrs. Buchanan experienced a frightening occurrence of haemorrhage shortly after she gave birth to a baby.

The medical doctor she visited for treatment advised her to take a mixture of 'Guinness stout' and egg. She was also advised to eat plenty of green vegetables. That potion the doctor told her, was to help in replacing lost blood. No scientifically appointed medication was prescribed in an effort to stop her heavy bleeding, then in its third day, Mrs. Buchanan naturally thought of visiting another doctor for better advice.

Her husband became deeply concerned about his wife's haemorrhaging over days. While at work, Mr. Buchanan related his wife's potentially dangerous condition to one of his good friends.

"Don't worry too much, man," his friend consoled, "I'll give you a remedy that will take care of the situation. Just get about a quarter or a tablet of 'laundry blue' and a large egg." He looked briefly at Mr. Buchanan and continued, "A table-spoonful of strong 'blue-water' must be mixed well with egg-white and orally taken by your wife..."

Mrs. Buchanan said that her husband reached home about 6 p.m. on that memorable day. He told her about the advice from his friend. He lost no time in doing as advised, for the sake of his wife.

Having taken the dose of that remedy she, not long after, fell asleep. She woke early next morning to discover that the haemorrhaging had ceased...completely.

Brain Tumour

Information concerning the following remedy came from a lady who claimed to have been cured by taking that simple remedy.

To experience a cure for such a significant problem that she described as a brain tumour by using a simple remedy, seems unbelievable.

However, she first commented on the several medical treatments she received over time yet no cure was experienced. At the end of her commentary she uttered, with much enthusiasm, the 'magic potion' that cured her from tumour of the brain.

The huge lady bent over forward and touched the periwinkle plant flowering at the front yard.

"Every day, boil four leaves to make a cup of tea from this plant," she said, "and now the doctor confirms that the tumour is gone."

She emphasised that only leaves taken from periwinkle plants that bear white flowers must be brewed for this remedy. Also, that no vessel or utensil made of aluminium should be used in the process.

Dog-Blood Brew

Miss Fodder told of what her doctor diagnosed as an infection of the bladder. She experienced a severe burning or pain down her vaginal track, she said. The burning became unbearable whenever she tried to urinate, which occurred too often in small amounts. Her doctor prescribed one large tablet, she said, along with an instruction for her to take orally, one half of the tablet first.

Instead of feeling relief by having taken the tablet, her condition literally worsened, explained Miss Fodder. During a conversation with a pharmacist whom she knew well, in Spanish Town, a different kind of tablet was brought to her without a doctor's prescription.

By having taken those tablets she experienced an appreciable relief from the painful condition. But basically the burning pain persisted in a sort of low-key manner.

Miss Fodder decided to see another doctor who, hopefully, would prescribe the appropriate medication for her woe. However, the expected costs of the doctor and pharmacy bills could be much higher than the amount of money that she would be able to produce.

It was the cost factor, which drove her to consider the use of folk medicine from a bush commonly called 'dog–blood'.

From her own experience Miss Fodder advises that the curative, antibiotic element of dog-blood can be decocted simply by boiling the bush in water for fifteen minutes. Should someone become similarly affected, she should drink a cupful of dog-blood brew in the morning and another at bedtime. Continue that dosage until the problem goes away.

Dog-blood brew is said also to be a proven remedy to flush out impurities from the reproductive systems of women, thus enabling them to become pregnant.

A Toddler's Dilemma

Mr. Bankley's two-year-old son was hospitalized as he suffered from diarrhoea and dehydration. The toddler remained in hospital, he said, for three months. However, the boy child was not responding sufficiently to medical treatment provided at the hospital.

In the rural parts of Jamaica, in particular, folks in sympathy with one's health problems usually give generously of their advice concerning remedies to be used as treatment for various illnesses.

It was an old lady who gave Mr. Bankley her advice of a remedy with which his son, who reached a near death condition, could be treated.

Mr. Bankley accepted her advice. He was allowed to administer the remedy to his toddler in the hospital. The folk treatment, said Mr. Bankley, had resulted in such a dramatic turn-around of the child's condition, that he became well enough to be taken home within five days of treatment.

The remedy was constituted of only two ingredients: a pint of pure honey and a comparable amount of olive oil.

Both ingredients were mixed.

The patient was given one tablespoonful of that mixture three times each day.

Today the former toddler patient, Mr. Bankley said, has reached twenty-three years of age at the time of writing this piece.

To Stop Bleeding Through the Nose

When a person experiences bleeding through the nose and no doctor or means of first-aid is available, what can be done to stop the bleeding?

The patient may at first attempt to plug the nostrils with cotton, toilet tissue, a bit of rolled fabric etc. Such methods may not be effective in getting the bleeding to stop in good time.

Folk advice says that in order to stop bleeding through the nose, a coin must be placed on the centre of the patient's forehead and firmly tied in place with a length of cloth or adhesive tape. Within a relatively short time bleeding through the nostrils will cease.

For Sweaty, Smelly Feet

After a day's work, play or other activities the feet of some people have sweated inside their shoes.

When sweaty feet are withdrawn from closed-up shoes they usually exude an odour that is less than pleasant.

Is there an easy, inexpensive way to treat smelly feet?

Folk doctors advise that before going out in the morning, for example, clean feet should be dusted (between toes, the soles, on top) with cornmeal before putting them into socks or shoes.

That act, it is said, will reduce or neutralize the bad odour that would otherwise have developed inside the shoes.

A Mysterious Cure

Reports of mysterious cures for illnesses abound. These cures are said to have manifested themselves without medical treatments.

A story of a mysterious cure has been told by a woman reminiscing on earlier years of her life. After five months in her pregnancy she experienced bleeding, apparently from her uterus.

During that stressful period she made regular visits to her gynaecologist and received prescribed medications in efforts to prevent or stop the continual bleeding.

She became very fearful that her pregnancy would have been aborted, as the medical treatments she received had not been effective in terminating the serious condition.

One day her female cousin, who lived some distance away, was passing by her home and paused to say a greeting. The cousin sensed her depressed mood and asked what was the cause.

Having then been told about the bleeding experienced by her cousin she gave advice that would seem untenable by sceptics.

Here is what the cousin advised: "Get your bible and pray Psalms 45, three times, over olive oil and drink it." Harbouring a residue of doubt about the workability of such a simplistic, dogmatic advice she, nevertheless, implemented the idea.

When later her doctor was told that the bleeding had effectively ceased through mysterious, non-medical means, he was stunned beyond belief.

Cured By Cow-Tongue

Mr. Dollison's story about a cure for his long lasting illness, through the use of a species of herb, is among many other stories told by others about herbal cures.

He told of pains and nausea he endured over several years as the result of an ulcerated stomach. The 'small fortune' he spent in doctors' fees and for prescribed medications could have been saved had he earlier known the simple curative remedy received through his recent acquaintance with an older lady.

This species of herb or bush has obviously derived its name, 'Cow-Tongue', from its leaves that resemble the long tongue of cows in terms of shape and the coarse texture of the leaves' top and under surfaces.

METHOD:

'Cow-tongue' leaves are narrow and long (12 inches or longer) and may need to be cut into bits before placing, say, three leaves into a pot with boiling water and allowing them to boil for 15-20 minutes. This process has to be repeated as the amount of brew therefrom must be taken by the patient, prior to bedtime, for nine consecutive nights; although relief from an ulcerated condition may materialize before the end of nine days as was Mr. Dollison's experience.

Sure Cure

Diarrhoea is a frequent intestinal evacuation of fluid stools. It can affect anyone, even animals. Many folk remedies have been recommended to treat this sickness.

Mrs. Bades has said that she recently had a severe case of diarrhoea. She went on to relate what she did to bring a quick end to that malady. Rather than hurrying off to consult a doctor for treatment, Mrs. Bades trusted in the home folk remedy that she had used previously with emphatic success in relieving herself of the diarrhoeal condition.

To prepare the remedy, Mrs. Bades garnered and grated five seeds of bissy (cola nuts). She placed the grated bissy outdoors so that heat from the sun would make them crisp.

It was thereafter put into a small pot of boiling water of appropriate amount for a strong brew when boiled. The decoction was made to boil for twenty minutes. After boiling, the resulting extract was strained and allowed to cool.

From that amount of bissy brew Mrs. Bades poured out a large cupful. Into that cupful of liquid she added two drops of essence-of-peppermint (it can be bought at the pharmacy without a doctor's prescription). Mrs. Bades then drank the cupful of that concoction. So effective was that remedy in terminating the diarrhoea that there was no need for her to ingest a second cupful.

Cured Through a Dream

Ms. Ramsay's story is not unique, though somewhat uncommon. She said that a week after she gave birth to a baby, some years ago, her face became swollen. She knew not why. With deep concern she visited her doctor to get a diagnosis of what had caused that painless swelling of her face.

The doctor ordered a medical test to determine the cause of her malady. Result of the test came out as negative. Next, she sought medical attention at the Kingston Public Hospital. Doctors at the hospital were unable to determine the cause of her swollen face.

Despite lack of certainty concerning the cause and nature of the swelling, a doctor, obviously by experience, prescribed medication that Ms. Ramsay was advised to ingest. After having taken the medication the swelling of her face disappeared and reappeared after the medication depleted.

Ms. Ramsay had not thought it wise to breastfeed her

infant child while she experienced that unexplained facial swelling. However, that scenario suddenly took an unexpected shift away from the physical level to a metaphysical realm when during sleep one night she got a dream.

During that dream Ms Ramsay was advised by a woman to use a certain herb that would resolve her problem. The folk name of the herb was 'georges-bush'. It was well-known to Ms. Ramsay.

Grown out of the ground, the long, slender, vine-like branches of georges-bush (also called chigger-knit bush, crocus-bush and yaws-bush) reach up variably from four to six feet in height. Its green leaves, the size of a palm of a small hand, carry wart-like lumps scattered over their top surface.

The 'dream lady' advised Ms. Ramsay to boil in water, for fifteen minutes, five leaves of georges-bush to make two cupfuls of reddish coloured brew that the leaves produced, with one dose to be taken orally in the morning and another cupful taken at bedtime.

As a result of having taken that dreamed-up remedy for nine days, the swelling of Ms. Ramsay's face disappeared then and never reappeared over more than twenty years up until today.

A Cure From Lignum Vitae

Mrs. Daphne Bennett shuddered in memory of the intermittent pains caused by tonsillitis, that she endured during part of her adolescent years of life – a long time ago, she insisted. She spoke of her visits to the doctor, the medication prescribed, the relief experienced, the resurgence of pain, and more visits to the doctor.

That painful circle persisted for more than two years, until one day a middle-aged man noticed her expressions of physical agony. When told that tonsillitis was causing the pain that she obviously was feeling, he hastened to offer her this advice:

"Go to de drug store, an' ask dem fe sell yuh a t'ing name 'lignum vitae gum'. When yuh go home yuh mus' bwile it inna water until 'de gum melt an' de whole t'ing tu'n to liquid. But don't drown out de gum wid too much water.

"When it done bwile, mek de liquid cool down but still as warm as yuh can bear it. Den yuh mus' use de liquid an' gargle yuh throat t'ree times a day wid it. Mi sure yuh gwine get relief, Miss Daphne."

Young Daphne then did as she was advised to do, and she confessed that after she did one gargle with the liquid, relief from the painful tonsils was experienced. Though more gargling ought to have been done, the relief she felt had so far, by just one dose of the mixture been permanent; lasting from that time up until today, over 50 years later, with no recurrence of tonsillitis.

Lignum vitae gum can be obtained directly from lignum vitae trees. Whenever lignum vitae trees sustain damage to the trunk, sap oozes out over time when it can be collected.

Treatment for Asthma

Asthma is a relatively common ailment affecting persons in all age groups. It is said to be an incurable disease, despite availability of modern scientific treatment.

But there are also folk medicinal treatments that are said to work sometimes more effectively than medical treatments.

One treatment known to work satisfactorily in treating asthma consists of only two ingredients: honey and garlic.

METHOD:

Get three heads of garlic and one quart of pure honey. Loosen the cloves of garlic from the heads. Place all the cloves into a suitable piece of fabric and use a wooden or metal bar to beat the garlic in the fabric to become a pulp.

Pour the honey into a suitable sized, wide-mouthed glass jar and plunge the beaten garlic therein.

Cover the mixture tightly into the jar and let stand in a cool place for a week to coalesce. That done, the patient of asthma should take a mouthful of the concoction before breakfast each morning and another mouthful at bedtime every day for at least nine consecutive days. As a result, relief from asthma in some cases, is long-lasting.

For Colds and Asthmatic Conditions

An advisor concerning herbal remedies has given an enthusiastic report about a kind of bush called 'fence-stake', so called because these evergreen, long-lasting trees are usually seen growing in a line with barbed-wire nailed to them as fencing.

These trees have a close resemblance to those that bear small plums called 'hog-plums'. Leaves taken from the fence-stake trees are reputed to be an effective treatment that reduces or eliminates the effects of chronic colds or asthma, particularly of children.

Boil a handful of the small leaves of fence-stake. An adult should take a cupful of the brew, and a smaller amount for a child. It should be taken each morning for nine consecutive mornings.

Fasten – Pon – Coat

The name 'fasten-pon-coat' depicts the nature of a wild herb so colloquially named. A plant of fasten-pon-coat grows up to about two feet above ground and has several branches, each anchored at the nodes or joints of the plant. The leaves of this small plant measure about 1½ inches across near the stems and taper down to pointed ends.

The plant has many green seeds, coated with skin that holds lots of tiny spikes that have the ability to stick on anyone whose clothes come in contact with them. Those seeds are unable to be taken off one's clothes without being crushed at the touch of one's fingers. The clinging residues of the seeds have to be scraped off one's garment. Nevertheless, fasten-pon-coat has medicinal potential.

Fasten-pon-coat when boiled in water produces a 'tea' that is an excellent remedy with which to treat anyone affected by vomiting or diarrhoea.

Velvet Treatment

'Velvet' is the folk name given to a wild growing vine that climbs upon small trees or shrubs found mainly in the country areas.

At each node of the vine, there grows usually one almost round leaf. The medicinal property of velvet can be decocted through the boiling of it in water.

The resulting brew should be taken orally as a proven remedy to treat ailments of the stomach, such as gastritis, ulcer, etc.

METHOD

About one quart of velvet brew should be bottled, placed into a refrigerator and used instead of water to quench one's thirst; the brew ought to be taken regularly throughout the day. None of the brew left overnight should be used the next day.

A fresh amount must be brewed and taken each day.

The consumption of brewed velvet should cover a period of nine consecutive days. Relief from problems of the stomach should then be pleasantly experienced.

Home Remedy for Coughing

A cough is an involuntary act of expelling air from the lungs suddenly with an explosive noise. It is sometimes accompanied by mucus coming up into the mouth.

Repeated coughing lasting over a period of say, a week or longer, can have a frustrating effect on the victim.

There is usually a need for treatment to enable an early relief from an unhealthy coughing.

The advice is to get a pint of pure honey and two large tubers of turnip. Place the turnip inside a jar and pour the honey therein.

Close the jar tightly and store in a cool place for two days, at least, to coalesce.

If no honey is available use instead a comparable amount of brown sugar. The juice exuding from the turnip will liquefy the sugar in the glass jar.

A mouthful of this concoction should be taken by the cough sufferer in the morning before breakfast, another mouthful taken at midday and yet another at bedtime.

Relief from coughing should be soon in coming.

Expel Gall-Stones

A remedy, said to be effective in expelling gall-stones from one's body has been given by folk advisors.

It is advised that one grapefruit or more should be peeled of its outer rind or 'skin'. The white pith around the fruit will then be exposed. That pith should be scraped off the fruit and placed into boiling water. Let it boil for 15 minutes. That process can be repeated as often as necessary. The resultant brew from boiling grapefruit pith should be taken daily until gall-stones have been expelled from one's body.

To Lose Excess Body Weight

Excess body weight has long been a serious human health hazard in Jamaica and other countries of the world.

Means of reducing body weight are several and various; some of those means work while others don't.

Some methods work for some persons and not for others.

An obese female friend of mine told of a method she used

which enabled her to lose 5 pounds of her body-weight within a week.

METHOD:
Mix one teaspoonful of vinegar with one cupful of hot water. Take one cupful of that mixture in the morning and another at bedtime. Repeat until loss of body-weight is experienced.

Treatment For Gum Boils

Gum boils are a common ailment. They are painful and prevent affected persons from eating comfortably. Persons do not always visit the doctor to get treatment for gum boils. Instead, they painfully wait until the boils break naturally.

The following homemade remedy usually works well to bring an early breaking of gum boils so that the accompanying pain ceases.

'Shame-lady' so-called, is a low lying plant that stretches an average of two feet, along the ground, away from its main root.

Along the vine of a shame-lady plant there are small sharp prickles and fine leaves at each node.

At the lightest touch of one's finger shame-lady's tiny leaves quickly withdraw and press themselves closely together as if hiding in shame of their 'nakedness'; hence the name, shame-lady.

METHOD:
To treat a gum boil: pull a shame-lady plant from the ground. Wash remnants of earth off its roots and place the uprooted plant (cut into bits if necessary) into a pot containing a pint of boiling lye-water (water mixed with a handful of ashes).

Let it boil for 20 minutes. When it has cooled down but is still highly warm, fill the mouth with the lye-water and hold it there for five minutes.

The remaining lye-water should be similarly used in two-hour intervals. Re-heat the mixture each time of usage. Expect an early breaking of the gum boil as the pus therein oozes out and causes relief.

Boils and Marigold

A boil is characterized as a localized swelling and inflammation of the skin resulting from infection in a skin gland. Having a hard central core, and forming pus. Boils can be painful throughout its period of infection which may last for a week or longer.

Should a boil be 'killed' as soon as it emerges or should it be allowed to develop and become a painful mound filled with pus that, in its own time, releases the pus and heals by itself? Almost any part of one's person can be affected by boils. At some parts of a person boil or boils can become extremely inconvenient for example, if it surfaces on the seat of one's buttocks. Sitting thus becomes a painful ordeal.

If the boil is newly emerging from one's skin or should it reach a more advanced stage of its development, the following remedy will expedite an end to it.

Marigold, commonly referred to as 'stinking-mary', is a common plant that is grown by gardeners for its bright, pleasant blooms, though its smell is less than pleasant. The method in treating boils starts when three leaves and two blooms are taken from a marigold plant. Place the leaves and blooms together into a clean piece of cloth, the size of a large handkerchief. After the ends of the fabric are held together, a piece of stick or metal should be used to pound the cloth containing the parts of marigold. The pounding facilitates extraction of its juice.

The beaten, wet marigold pulp must be used to smear generously the 'young' boil that soon after will disappear, or the developed boil will timely release all its pus and pain.

To Treat the Flu

Influenza (flu) is a common ailment. It is at times accompanied by fever, runny nose and sometimes pain at parts on one's person.

Those affected by the flu usually want to get rid of the nauseating, uncomfortable feelings experienced thereby.

Nowadays, there are choices of different types of medications that can be bought at the pharmacy without a doctor's prescription to treat the flu.

But, even with easy access to modern medication, many persons still turn to cultural folk medicines used at the first symptoms of the flu. People turn to traditional remedies for two main reasons: remedies are usually cheaper to obtain than prescribed medicines and some remedies work as effectively as scientifically produced medication.

The following is a remedy given by Mr. Williams who said he had used it to treat an attack of the flu. It showed astonishing effectiveness in terms of fast relief from symptoms of influenza.

The two ingredients needed to make this remedy are easily obtained in almost every neighbourhood in Jamaica. The following concoction may not be taken by children or persons with medical conditions that could be adversely affected by it.

At any rum bar, buy a drink of pure white rum. Add to the rum a level teaspoonful of finely powdered black-pepper. Mix both ingredients and take the mixture orally. Relief, is said, will come quickly.

A Clue for the Flu

There is enough scientifically formulated medication available to treat influenza, yet many persons persist in the use of folk remedies to treat it. Is it because they achieve the healing sought from remedies?

Out of many folk treatments recommended for the flu, the following remedy is said to be effective and is likely to cost little or nothing in contrast to a doctor's bill.

METHOD:

Get, say, two large fresh Seville oranges also called 'sour' oranges. Squeeze the juice out of both oranges into a teacup. Clean water amounting to a third of the amount of juice, must be poured into the juice.

To that mixture, add a level tablespoonful of brown sugar, not in order to sweeten the 'sour' orange juice but because sugar is considered to be an essential ingredient for this concoction. Stir the liquid with a spoon until the sugar has melted.

A person afflicted by the flu is advised to drink such a substance to experience, not only relief from the flu, but possibly a return of lost appetite for food.

Treatment for 'Bad Belly'

Personal testimonies from people who experience cures for illnesses through non-medical treatment give authenticity to the use of folk remedies and advice.

Here is a case of a woman who, according to her story, has for more than ten years suffered continual chronic belly pains, despite numerous prescribed treatments she had taken from medical doctors.

'Bad belly' is the folk diagnosis of such a complaint. Relief came from those perennial pains when that woman accepted advice from a folk 'doctor'.

She was advised to reap three different kinds of wild growing herbs, namely: 'guinea-hen-weed', 'fasten-pon-coat' and 'fox-tail-grass' (used with roots intact).

METHOD:

The three kinds of herbs must be boiled together into a quart of water for twenty minutes. Thereafter, two table spoonfuls of 'cobweb' (created by frequent wood-fire smoke going up to the roof inside an old-time kitchen) should be scraped off and mixed with the boiled brew.

The patient should take a mouthful of that concoction every six hours. Despite its bitterish taste, a relief from 'bad belly' pains should be attained in good time.

The process may be repeated if necessary.

To Combat Hypertension

An acquaintance of mine has been through a painful experience with a headache that, he says, had lasted for over a month of daily pain. A nurse, living in the same district as he, offered to test his blood pressure. The blood pressure monitor indicated that the man's blood pressure was dangerously high.

The nurse advised him to see the doctor who held a clinic every Tuesday at the health centre. But on Saturday the man received advice from a friend who offered a simple remedy to treat his hypertension.

His friend instructed him to pick a white cho-cho from the cho-cho harbour at his back-yard. He was thereafter advised to pick two large, mature limes from a nearby tree.

METHOD:
Grate the cho-cho, he was told, and squeeze the liquid out of the grated stuff into a container. Cut the limes and squeeze the juice out of them into the juice of the cho-cho and drink the mixture.

An hour after he drank that concoction, he says his headache ceased. However, on Tuesday at the clinic, he was tested by the doctor who advised him that his blood pressure was safely normal.

Since then, two years hence, he says he has not had a recurrence of that hypertension headache.

Against Hypertension

I know of no other illness that attracts a higher number of folk remedies than the many recommended as treatment for hypertension or high blood pressure.

The use of the juice brewed from breadfruit leaves boiled into water is reputed to work well by way of causing relief from high blood pressure that has long become a scourge in Jamaica and elsewhere.

The following is a remedy that has been used by some folks to treat high blood pressure. It has come from Ms. E. Anglin-Wright who said that she learnt about it from her grandmother who lived to the ripe old age of 102 years.

In the grandmother's lifetime she was affected by hypertension. She had continually boiled breadfruit leaves in water, bottled the resultant brew and drank from it when necessary – even when thirsty, as an effective treatment with which she managed to maintain a stable, safe blood pressure, according to her granddaughter.

But there is more to it. The simple process of making this potion had taken an air of mystery as Ms. Anglin-Wright explains that the breadfruit leaves to be used in this decoction must not drop from the tree directly to the ground.

Leaves to be used must be allowed to yellow and detach themselves naturally, at maturity, and fall from the tree. The green leaves are not thought suitably raised above ground and must be put in place underneath the breadfruit tree to catch falling ripe leaves to be used for such a purpose.

Relief From Diarrhoea

Among the many folk remedies for relief from diarrhoea is the use of leaves taken from star-apple trees.

METHOD:
Simply place seven leaves plucked from a star-apple tree, into boiling water.

Let them boil for 15 minutes. Take the resulting 'tea' without sweetening.

The dosage may be repeated if the diarrhoea does not cease within the same day.

Infant's Diarrhoea

Remedies used as treatment of diarrhoea affecting adults may not be used to treat the tender digestive or excretory system of infant children.

In the olden days, castor oil, guava buds, search-me-heart and several other remedies were used effectively to combat diarrhoea mainly in adults.

However, diarrhoea affecting infants was treated with milder remedies. One mild remedy was the water taken from very young coconuts and fed to infants so affected. Regular checks on the infants' condition would show expected improvement in good time.

Against Diarrhoea

There are several different kinds of folk remedies designed to treat occurrence of diarrhoea in people. Among those remedies that have worked well, then and now, is one that can be made by using three ingredients: wheaten flour, water and a pinch of salt.

METHOD:

Place about one half ($\frac{1}{2}$) pound of flour into a heated vessel over low fire. Keep stirring the flour while it progressively burns and becomes brown in colour. At this stage, the vessel holding the burnt flour should be taken off the fire.

Next, pour a common sense amount of clean water on the burnt flour into the container. Add the salt to the mixture until it attains the consistency of ordinary porridge.

The patient of diarrhoea should drink the whole dose (about a cupful) at once, with the certainty that if no other disease underlies the diarrhoea being treated he/she will shortly be relieved of the diarrhoea condition.

Treatment For Diarrhoea

Although their prevalence has diminished drastically over the several decades past, folk remedies are still used today, particularly in the country parts of Jamaica.

The choice of using folk remedy rather than using scientific medication to treat an illness is sometimes dictated by the cost factor. Medication prescribed by a doctor often costs more money than most people can afford. Home-brewed remedies may cost little or nothing at all. For example, the following remedy is one of many folk remedies that may be used to treat diarrhoea.

METHOD:

Get one pomegranate (commonly called pranganate). Cut this fruit open and deposit the parts into a small pot containing three cupfuls of boiling water. Let boiling continue for fifteen minutes. After boiling, straining (if necessary) and cooling, the addition of sugar is optional.

The person affected by diarrhoea is advised to drink one cupful of the boiled pomegranate-water and take the rest of the drink four hours later, if necessary.

If there exists no underlying disease to nullify the 'pomegranate treatment', relief from diarrhoea is said to be guaranteed.

Surgery Not Necessary

If certain parts of one's body or limbs have been deeply pierced by say a thorn, splintered glass bottle, a bullet from a gun, etc., the need for surgery done by a doctor might not be necessary to extract any foreign matter involved.

An application of biscuits or crackers can be used instead of surgery.

This method of extraction as given by 'underworld practitioners' is used by those persons, particularly in the crimefields. It is said to be consistently effective in extracting bullets from persons who refuse to go to the hospital or doctor, through fear of being apprehended by the police for involvement in wrong-doings.

METHOD:

The biscuit or biscuits must be thoroughly soaked into water. Use the soaked biscuit as a poultice applied directly to the wounded part of the body or limb. Use also a wrap of fabric or adhesive tape to hold the poultice in place.

The foreign matter, it is claimed, will, over time, be drawn up to the surface of the wound from where it can be easily removed.

Folk Ways, Means and Things

Cook Without Pot And Water

In long gone decades of post-slavery times, farmers in the lofty hills of Sligoville, St. Catherine, cleared parts of the forest around, where they cultivated crops such as several species of yam, different types of cocoa, varieties of sweet potato, corn, red peas, gungo peas, cassava, pumpkins, etc.

Sawyers, too, felled timber trees with which they made board and roofing shingles, done at prepared sites in the forest. They sometimes remained in the forest working for up to a week at a time before they returned home.

During that process of working in the forest, far from home, farmers as well as sawyers, have had to prepare daily meals for themselves at their work places.

However, they sometimes experienced a big problem: that of having not enough water with which to cook their foodstuff each day, and attend to matters of hygiene during long, severe droughts when the hillside farmers cleared land, but waited for rainfall before planting crops.

Having had no river – not even a small spring, piped water was virtually unheard of within a radius of five miles – the area had to be watered solely by rainfall which, at times was absent for many a month.

Folks back then have had, regularly, to take the long, hazardous trek to reach the far away river to fill one tin pan of water, carried on their heads to reach back home. A person or persons in a group of water carriers would sometimes trip and fall, thus wasting the precious little water at part of the way home.

Whenever there was not enough water to cook with, work-men in the forest were forced, by necessity, to devise another way of cooking without using more than the barest minimum of water.

In order to cook foodstuff without using pot and water done in contrast to the traditional way, the workmen would dig into the ground a hole of say, twelve inches deep and eighteen inches square more or less, or according to the amount of stuff to be placed into it.

Quailed banana fronds or leaves were used to seal the hole in its entirety. The leaves protruding upwards out of the hole would later be bent over to help cover the hole in the air-resistant way. But before that time, a small amount of water, one pint perhaps, was poured into the bottom of the leaf-paved hole. With the foodstuff then placed into the hole, the upward protruding parts of the leaves, were bent over to help cover the hole. Additional banana leaves (cocoa leaves can also be used) would be used to reinforce the covering, so that it would bear the weight of the modest layer of earth placed on top of it. The leaves were arranged to prevent droppings of earth into the cooking chamber below. On top of the layer of earth a 'lively' fire was created and fuelled by wood or charcoal.

The foodstuff placed into the hole would be steam-cooked and ready for eating earlier than when cooked in a pot and water.

Finding enough water to drink was problematic as well. But those resourceful workmen, at that time in our history, reaped water-wiss (withe) in the forest and sucked enough water from it to quench their thirst, particularly after having eaten cooked ground provisions and huge flour-dumplings garnished, perhaps, with thirst-creating salted fish or pickled meat.

Crocus Bags

Many decades ago much larger volumes of sugar were produced in Jamaica than the amounts produced today.

Such large volumes of sugar manufactured then, required correspondingly large quantities of crocus bags to contain sugar for export and for use locally.

Crocus bags were thick, coarse and closely knitted. When emptied of sugar the bags were eagerly sought after by country farmers, especially those who utilized them in different ways.

In those days crocus bags were virtually indispensable to small farmers in the country parts. The bags were mainly used for moving goods to and from farms deep into the forests.

The bags were also tailored to make knapsacks that were hung over farmers' shoulders in carrying small or personal items. Crocus material was derived from jute.

Apparently, because of the nature of the material from which the bags were made, they generated much heat inside of them. Washed and dried, crocus bags were also an important bedding material in the homes of many a peasant folk back then in slavery and post-slavery times. Stuffed with a selected kind of grass called cotton-grass and having its open end sewn up, a crocus bag then became a mattress to sleep on. Many children, who under such circumstances in those days, usually slept underneath the beds of their parents, kept themselves assuredly warm, during the coldest of weather by having had the full length of their bodies pushed into crocus bags provided as bedding for nighttime sleep. However, crocus bags have long been replaced by bags made of other materials, such as nylon, to contain sugar.

Roofing Shingles

Long ago shingles produced for roofing were in widespread use all over Jamaica. Production of shingles in those days was fraught with hard work.

The easiest part, perhaps, was to identify suitable trees in the forest.

For most shingles-makers cedar was the wood of choice for roofing. Cedar shingles were long-lasting against hostile elements and relatively soft to work with.

The real back-breaking work began when, for example, an agile man wielded an axe to hack, (sometimes for several hours) at the trunks of chosen trees in order for them to fall.

In many cases, the place where the falling trees would drop was pre-determined by the axe wielder. In case of a cultivated area nearby, the tree must be made to fall away from the cultivation.

That was done by deeply cutting into the tree's trunk almost entirely at one side facing where the tree was expected to fall. However, when the tree's trunk was deeply cut it became extremely vulnerable to any puff of wind that could topple it over to fall on the opposite side and damage the cultivation.

If, fortunately, the tree fell at the place intended, then came the next stage of the work – to de-limb the fallen tree. That de-limbing process, having been done, there was yet another stage of the work which needed the help of a second person to operate the crosscut saw in cutting the stock of timber into blocks of about two feet for the length of shingles to be made.

The idea of moving those weighty blocks of aromatic cedar wood to the site of a house under construction was futile indeed when faced with, say a one-mile labourious trip up and down treacherous foot-tracks along rough, inhospitable terrain. Shingles, therefore, had to be made on the spot in the forest.

Each block of wood was put to stand on end at a level spot of ground. The shingle maker then measured across the surface of the block's upper end and marked lines of about a quarter of an inch apart that represented the thickness of each shingle when split off the block.

A metal tool called 'fro' having had a thin edge, a thick back ridge and handles, was lined up with each mark and held there while another person, using a weighty club of wood, struck with full strength, the back ridge of the fro.

A shingle would spring off the block by time the fro was struck to half-way down the block of timber.

That process was repeated hundreds or thousands of times according to the need in terms of the size building to be roofed.

When that phase of the work was done, a donkey, mule or head-load would be used to move the rough shingles to the site of building where they would be 'dressed' or shaved by using a sharp implement called a 'drawing knife'.

The person dressing or shaving the shingles had to sit on a wooden contraption called a 'horse'. With the shaver's feet out-stretched they kept in place a lever that held down each shingle to the horse. Each shingle was placed in a flat position to be shorn of its roughness and given smooth surfaces.

The drawing knife had a very sharp blade with handles that curved inwards at both ends which enabled the drawing knife to be pushed forth and drawn back, shaving off the shingles.

From start to finish, producing shingles by the old time method took a long time to be done in such a strenuous way.

Today, however, with the use of modern machines, producing shingles or any other wood-based amenity, now takes a mere fraction of the time and physical energy expended by our fore-bears.

Lest we forget...

Those Beasts of Burden

Mules seem to be almost extinct in Jamaica. Many decades ago there was a population of those animals in every parish of the island.

But as modern means of moving goods and people became more and more accessible, over time, there has been less and less need for the slow moving, so-called, beasts of burden.

The population of donkeys also has dwindled considerably. Formerly reliable carriers of goods and persons, mules and donkeys were greatly valued animals particularly in deep rural areas, characterized by rough, hilly and steep terrain.

In the days of old almost every country farmer owned a mule or donkey. But today those animals are rarely seen any-where.

Donkeys were amazingly hardy and sure-footed, while mules were known for their strength in transporting weighty produce from farm to market and so on.

The fact that mules don't reproduce their species might also have contributed to their steep numerical decline. A mule was propagated by way of mating a female donkey with a stud horse. Ironically, when a male donkey was mated with a female horse, the off-spring that resulted was of a different species of animal called 'mule-royal'.

Donkeys would take thirteen months to reproduce but they were of a fairly docile nature; quite unlike mules that tended to be 'temperamental'.

When disturbed by other animals or by humans who handled them, mules sometimes inflicted serious injuries, even fatal ones, at times, to unsuspecting persons.

Care had to be taken when approaching some mules in order to avoid their mighty kicks or aggressive bites. Yet, some mules were comparatively gentle to handle.

Horses, always admired and exploited for their grace and speed in galloping, have managed to survive in more numbers than mules and donkeys, mainly through their suitability for commercial racing.

But even so there are much fewer horses today than during slavery and post-slavery times when they were routinely ridden on plantations, put to haul buggies, to race, and to turn mills for the grinding of sugar cane.

If nothing is done to preserve the existence of mules and donkeys, within a few decades to come posterity will be served only through words and pictures of those once invaluable animals.

About 'Pissilly' Bird

A small species of bird with attractive yellow and black plumes, commonly called 'Pissilly', invariably builds its nest in very close proximity to hives of wasps. Folks say that its close affinity with vicious wasps guarantees the bird's protection against possible predators, invaders or other intruders that may want to molest its eggs, young ones or itself.

How Not to Break an Egg

The fragility of an egg is well known. It may be broken by a mere pressured touch of one's finger.

Yet, in an instant, it can be made to withstand tremendous pressure and not break at all.

How? Place an egg (poultry) between both palms. Also, place both ends of the egg in a left-to-right position.

Interlock the fingers and press inwards hand to hand, steadily.

Even the strongest person may not be able to crush an egg that way.

Jack Panya Chicken

Before the modern 'hybrid' poultry was developed, folks particularly in the country areas reared fowls usually called 'common fowl'.

Occasionally, one out of a brood of chickens hatched by a hen would curiously appear without any feathers whatsoever. The chicken would grow to become an 'adult' fowl with a completely bare body.

That phenomenon was called 'Jack Panya Fowl'; hence the long existing colloquialism which says:

"Jack Panya no pray fe feather
Him only ask fe long life."

Cling-Cling

The bird known as cling-cling is also called 'jumper'. It sometimes feeds on the ground and gets about by jumping with long, reddish feet.

As a timid, dirurnally oriented species, this darkly coloured bird will quickly fly out of situations that seem to threaten its safety or invade its space.

A noticeable feature of this bird's existence is its ability (despite its diurnal nature) to make a straight streak of flight from point A to point B at night, while making loud calls of "cling-cling-cling..."

Some folks in these deep rural parts express the belief that the bird's nocturnal flights qualify them as 'duppy birds'. But deeper thought reflects the possibility that birds of the cling-cling species sometimes have to make emergency flights at night in order to escape from attacks by predators such as rats that can invade their habitat; therefore the birds ought not to be unfairly classified as 'duppy birds'.

Cats

Whenever a domestic cat is held aloft, turned upside down, and allowed to fall back down first, it never falls on its back. The agile creature does a split-second flip over in mid-air and lands on its feet.

On the subject of cats: what happens to cats when they become too old to live any longer? Some folks say that old cats don't die; instead, they naturally wander off into the forest or other similar settings and are mysteriously transformed to become owls...believe it or not.

The facial resemblance of cats and owls might have given rise to such an apparent myth.

Sprat Fish

It is worth knowing that a species of popularly eaten fish called 'sprat' becomes soft in its total make-up during the new-moon phase. In fact, too soft to be caught by fisher-folk at sea using a hook and line, as told by informants.

Yampie

All varieties of the yam family sprout vines that climb up spirally on stakes or nearby trees.

In the process of climbing up, all species of yam vines climb by wrapping themselves from right to left around the stakes.

However, there is one species of yam with vines that climbs in the opposite way by going from left to right around the stakes. That species of yam is called 'Yampie'.

Why Star Apples?

Does it help to know that star apples, when cut diametrically, show the bright imprint formed in the likeness of a star at the centre of the apples – hence the name star apple?

The "C" in Breadfruit

The letter 'C' can be found inside the stem of every breadfruit. In order to see the marvellous C, the stem of a breadfruit, for example, must be cut horizontally.

The 'C' is seen at both cut-ends of the stem.

It is believed by some folks that breadfruit had been eaten by Christ who, thereafter, miraculously imprinted the initial letter of his name into the stem as a token of his gastronomic satisfaction.

Bamboo Blossom

Several persons consulted said they have never seen bamboo in bloom. Is it that bamboo does not flower at all?

The answer seems to be that bamboo blooms only at night. It is said that collecting fallen bamboo blossoms during the night, provides a powerful component in the craft articulated by some practitioners of the occult.

Hog–Doctor

There is a species of trees known as 'hog-doctor'.

Some such trees can be seen at Stanbury Grove and Mount Moreland districts in the sprawling hilly Sligoville area of St. Catherine.

Hog-doctor produces an acidic sap or juice. Farmers, in particular those who at times must cut away these relatively small 5-7 foot tall trees in order to clear ground for farming, must exercise care in handling such trees lest they sustain acidic burns by the juice exuding from the cut or bruised parts of these trees.

But even without cuts and bruises, hog-doctor can cause injury to anyone in harm's way.

For example, an unwary person who may come in close contact with a hog-doctor tree during rainfall is likely to be burned by acid-tainted rain-water coming off the small leaves of the tree; so potent is its acidic content!

Couldn't commercial acid be developed from hog-doctor?

Only a scientific study of hog-doctor could furnish an answer.

Horse-Eye Nuts

The nuts, called horse-eye nuts, conceivably derived this name from their resemblance of the eyes of a horse.

Round along the periphery, somewhat flat at both sides, these smooth, chocolate coloured nuts are hard to crack because of their toughness.

The nuts have kernels inside but they are not considered as edible, though reputed as having medicinal potential.

The vine of a horse-eye plant climbs up on small nearby trees and produces nuts enclosed in pods. At maturity, the pods open and allow the nuts to fall to the ground in continuum with the cycle of their reproduction.

Popular many decades ago, among boys in the rural areas, horse-eye nuts were played with in the same way that foreign-made marbles were used in games by boys in the town parts.

But the more important use that was made of horse-eye nuts in those days was as a sort of coolant. Long before refrigerators and manufactured ice were known, people sought ways to keep water as cool as possible for the purpose of drinking.

The well-known 'Spaniard jars' and other types of jars made of clay, in different sizes and shapes, were commonly used in an effort to keep drinking water at a low temperature.

Back then, only a few jars perhaps would be found in a typical country neighbourhood without three to six or more horse-eye nuts (depending on the size of the jar) resting at the bottom for the purpose of keeping the water very cool for drinking.

If the water became contaminated by whatever kind of foreign matter, the nuts would burst open and float.

Lest we forget...

Pimento

Pimento, also called allspice, is a traditional crop in Jamaica. It had for long been experienced that pimento would not grow when the seeds were sown by farmers nor would young plants grow when transplanted.

Pimento then, existed through propagation by birds that fed on ripe pimento berries and excreted the seeds during flight or at perch. The seeds would fall to the ground, germinate, grow and become additional pimento trees growing at unselected places over the countryside.

Science, however, intervened and made the propagation of pimento through available seedlings, a commonplace activity that today occurs at selected places.

As a spice and a seasoning for meats, soups etc., pimento is well used in Jamaica and elsewhere. But little known is the fact that old time folk used pimento to provide heat as well. For example, in order to have, say, plantains, banana or avocado quickly ripened to be ready on time for market day, a farmer would gather an appropriate amount of dried banana fronds, put them out to warm in the sun and thereafter stuff them into a barrel along with a similar amount of pimento leaves.

The fruits intended to be ripened were subsequently placed into the barrel and inter-stuffed with the medium to retain heat. The barrel, when closed, over time, would hold a significant build-up of heat. That heat forced the fruits to ripen in much less time than they normally would.

Also, a person might not long endure staying in, say, a room with stored pimento without becoming dehydrated by the effects of heat therefrom.

Many years ago, as a boy growing up in a pimento producing mountain village, I overheard my elders saying that pimento was also used at that time to pad the uniforms of soldiers, as it helped to keep them warm during cold weather on the battlefields abroad.

To Find the Leaking Part

In order to find leakage of water going through an undetected hole or crack in a tank, swimming pool etc., simply drop a light 'English' cork into the water remaining therein. The floating cork will soon position itself and settle directly above the leaking part of the water's container.

A feather may also be used for the same purpose.

Did You Know

...that pork, when placed in hot sunshine for hours, breeds maggots?

...that green susumber 'berries' have a bitterish taste when cooked but if allowed to ripen on the tree they develop a sweet taste?

...that peppermint, when reaped and used at midnight, can be toxic?

...that donkeys and horses take 13 months to give birth?

...that mules do not reproduce because they do not mate sexually?

...that the hairless round scars seen at the inner sides of a donkey's upper front legs are said to be finger marks made by Christ's touch when he indicated his blessing of the ass for safely taking him to his destination?

...that if a male horse has unknowingly been mated with its mother, it will, on finding out, rip away its genitals by using its teeth and subsequently suffer death?

...that a female goat will eat the placenta that passes out after giving birth to its offsprings?

...that the relatively large Jamaican green lizards changes their colour at will, from green and black to green again...and that the male green lizard has a serrated ridge along its back which it uses on rare occasions, to saw off a small limb or to fell a small tree?

...that the plant called 'basil' will keep flies out of the house if placed near windows?

...that if too much salt accidentally gets into a pot of food being cooked the salt content can be diminished by placing a green tomato into a pot?

...that a wild growing plant called 'jack-in-the-bush', if regularly used to make 'tea' to drink causes erectile dysfunction or impotence in men?

...that Sligoville, in the parish of St. Catherine, Jamaica, was the first Free Village established in Jamaica in the year 1835; that it was also the first Free Village established in the West Indies and that it was the first Free Village established in the entire Western Hemisphere?

Jamaican Proverbs

Jamaican proverbs or sayings portray tenets of Jamaica's culture meaningfully expressed. The survival of these gems seems secure, based on their survival over many decades past. The following are proverbs that have spanned the ages and yet remain relevant in today's world.

Idle donkey follow cane trash go a pound.
Meaning:
Following trifles too far can lead one into serious trouble.

If yuh mek yuh bed hard yuh haffi lie down hard.
Meaning:
If one uses the wrong method, one must expect the wrong outcome.

From saltfish a shingle house top.
Meaning:
Something that has been happening for a very long time.

A nuh want of tongue mek cow nuh talk.
Meaning:
It is not that one does not know the secret, but it is unwise to reveal it.

Rain a fall but de dutty tough.
Meaning:
In the midst of plenty one gets little or nothing.

Long road brings sweat but short-cut brings blood.
Meaning:
Take enough time to do things right; the shorter way could be fraught with dangers unseen.

Dog a sweat but long hair cover it.
Meaning:
A troubled mind is covered with a bright smile.

Cuss de devil but give him what's due.
Meaning:
Even a bad person who does a good deed ought to be commended.

Ashes cold, dog sleep in deh.
Meaning:
Unlike past times, one becomes helpless while others take unfair advantage.

Once a man, twice a child.
Meaning:
Helplessness, usually associated with old age, is compared with a state of childhood or infancy.

The pig asked mother hog: "Mumma wha' mek yuh mout' so long?"
Mother hog replied: "Yuh a grow up, mi pickney, yuh soon see yuh own mout'."
Meaning:
Some physical features and behaviour don't occur early in life but will later emerge.

De higher monkey climb, de more him expose himself.
Meaning:
Upward social mobility through secret dishonest means will sooner or later be exposed.

Don't mek grass grow under yuh foot.
Meaning:
Don't procrastinate. Do it now.

Today fi yuh tomorrow fi mi.
Meaning:
Don't humiliate me because of your achievement today. My day of achievement will also come.

If yuh live inna glass house don't throw stones.
Meaning:
Don't criticise others if your lifestyle is vulnerable to 'to throw-back' criticism.

The older the moon the brighter it shines.
Meaning:
Older persons may still perform better than many.

If yuh doh done climb the hill don't throw 'way yuh walking stick'.
Meaning:
You may fall short of your goal if you abandon, too soon, those who supported you in reaching thus far.

Never bite the hands that feed you.
Meaning:
Don't ever abuse or be ungrateful to those who served you well.

Mother has, father has but blessed is the child who has his/her own.
Meaning:
Set not your heart on things that parents possess; go, seek your own.

Penny wise but pound foolish.
Meaning:
Great attention is given to minor things while the important matters are ignored.

Let sleeping dogs lie.
Meaning:
Don't raise a highly contentious matter without a big reason.

Rolling stones gather no moss.
Meaning:
Continually moving from place to place leaves little time to accumulate worthwhile possessions.

Beauty is only skin deep.
Meaning:
Deeper beauty can shine out from one's inner being.

Not all that glitters is gold.
Meaning:
Proposals or promises may seem excellent but beneath is planned deception or disappointment.

He who lives the longest will see the most...
Meaning:
Only an unspecified period of time and experience will bring the answers sought.